# THE FIREPROOF TEACHER

## SEVEN STRATEGIES FOR PREVENTING TEACHER BURNOUT

### BY JOHN SPENCER

Date of First Publication: March 17, 2015

**Wren Media**
P.O. Box 5970
Glendale, AZ 85312
United States of America

ISBN: 978-0692410547

## DEDICATION

To the teachers:
Thank you for all that you do.

# TABLE OF CONTENTS

# Preface
## We Don't Need Rock Stars

I used to hate reading education books because I always felt like crap afterward. (Am I allowed to use the word "crap" in an education book?) There were always seven steps and eight keys on an endless journey toward perfection. After awhile, I felt like a custodian on a Stairmaster, struggling to keep my keys together and exhausted by all the steps.

It was more than that, though. I would read these books and it rarely squared with my reality as a teacher. One pundit told me that if I just had my crap together (see, I used it again) on my first day of my first year I wouldn't have any discipline issues ever. That's right. Teachers can be deeply effective from the first day they walk into the classroom. Another man told me that if I just instituted a set of fifty-one rules, kids would be great. That's right. Fifty-one. That's a solid forty-one more than the list from Moses. I remember reading about the utopian classrooms that these pundits described and I'd wonder what was wrong with me.

When would I get to that place as a teacher?

Well, here I am eleven years later and I don't have the perfect classroom. I'm not one hundred percent effective from day one. I don't have all the answers. I haven't won any major teaching awards, though my peanut butter chews won a close second place in the all-staff holiday dessert contest.

And yet, here I am in my eleventh year of teaching and I still drive to work each day feeling content. I still enjoy what I'm doing.

I know, I know. We're supposed to be martyrs. We're supposed to be telling everyone how hard this gig is (and don't get me wrong, there are tough moments) but I'm actually having the time of my life. (Note to readers: if the words, "time of my life" suddenly make you think of Patrick Swayze then you might just be a child of the eighties).

## Kids Don't Need Rock Star Teachers

The bottom line is this: I'm not a rock star teacher. I can't sell you a snake-oil program that will guarantee your students will pass all of the high-stakes tests. I don't work miracles. My teardrops don't cure leprosy. I still have lessons that tank. I still have moments that are cringe-worthy. Just a month ago I embarrassed a kid in front of the class and had to flag him down after school to apologize.

I'm not a rock star . . . but what if I were? I thought about this one morning after hearing the words "rock star" thrown around to describe great teachers. It had me wondering what an actual rock star would be like in the classroom. Here are a few ideas we all came up with (check out the version on Storify at https://storify.com/acampbell99/rock-star-teachers).

- Rock star teacher demands that all the green M&Ms be removed from the staff lounge candy bowl.
- Rock star teacher asks students to pay for her autograph when writing a hall pass.
- Rock star teacher assumes the fight breaking out by the door is simply a lively mosh pit.
- Rock star teacher teaches pass the bell and calls it an "encore presentation."

- Rock star teacher refers to the supply cabinet as the "merchandise booth."
- Rock star teacher is perpetually disappointed when he jumps off the desk but none of the kindergarteners will crowd-surf him.
- Rock star teacher refers to the laser pointer and SMART Board as the "amazing laser and light show."
- After the warm-up, rock star teacher tosses a sweaty rag at the students and proceeds to pour a bottle of water over his face.
- Rock star teacher gets so excited about linear equations that she has been known to set the erasers on fire.
- Rock star teacher refers to the custodial staff as "roadies" and the student teacher as a "backup singer."
- Rock star teacher allows students to wave lighters in the air during a very emotional reading of *Green Eggs and Ham*
- We knew we were in trouble when rock star teacher said, "This is Yoko. She'll be attending all of our department meetings from now on."

Kids don't need rock stars. They're not looking for adults with accolades and notoriety. They need

humble, approachable teachers who care deeply about them. They need teachers who are passionate about the subject and have a blast teaching it.

You know who they need? They need someone like Phyllis. You've probably never heard of her because she has never sought out the limelight. She was the art teacher at my school for thirty years and then she retired . . . for a summer. Now she's teaching computers in the room next to me. There will never be a movie made about her career. She may never be a coveted keynote speaker at a massive conference.

However, there are thousands of students whose lives have been radically changed because she created a safe place for creativity to thrive. She has been doing that everyday for decades.

She could have been a rock star smashing guitars and performing for packed arenas but instead she created an acoustic jam session that put the spotlight on the students while she quietly changed lives. That's why ultimately I want to be more like Phyllis and less like a rock star.

## No Magic Formulas

There are no magic formulas to fix teacher burnout. I mention this because I looked for a something fast and easy and practical when I was in the midst of my worst year of teaching. I wanted a snake oil solution that would make things better. I never found it.

Instead, I watched teachers around me who had lasted. All of these teachers had experienced rough spots. They had been through times when they wanted to quit. However, they didn't. I learned from their example. I noticed strategies they used to continue thriving on their worst days. That's really what this book is about. It's based upon the strategies I have seen from the passionate veteran teachers who have kept the flame in the midst of tough situations.

If you're a teacher that's having a rough year, my hope is that you will connect with some of these strategies. My hope is that you'll find a place where you love going to work again. My hope is that you'll be fireproof.

# The Burnout Epidemic

He tightens his tie, but it is still an inch and a half below the belt. Carefully looping each knot once again, he feels the sense of ritual slipping through his hand. As he steps back, the tie leans slightly.

"I'll let it walk with a limp," he tells himself.

He studies the flickering gray hairs by his sideburns. No one told him gray hair would be the norm at thirty-three. He stares into the mirror. Wrinkled lines on his forehead, a tie suffocating his ability to breath. Suffocation. That's it. The ritual itself is suffocating. It's all become a meaningless ritual. They stripped away his name, gave him a title, told him to wear professional clothing and now he is nothing more than a number on a graph.

*I'm a phony in a Cathedral of Data. I'm a participant in an institution that I can no longer love. It's not that I don't believe in learning. I just don't believe in school anymore.*

He gathers up his backpack, water bottle and lunch box. He daydreams about the Star Wars Thermos he used to fill up as a child.

"I used to love learning. I used to love school. I used to love teaching," he whispers to himself.

He thinks back to the first few years, when he would set up his class two weeks earlier than the rest of the staff. He would make lists and lists of lists and he'd play an old vinyl record of Pink Floyd as a sort-of ritual reminding him of his childhood and the shag carpet and the new hope that came with the start of every school year. He would move desks around and hang up posters and tell himself that this year would be the best ever.

This year, though, the backpack feels heavier and like his tie, he walks with slumped shoulders. He hopes with a limp. *I will endure four hours of meaningless PowerPoint presentations. I will learn, yet again, how to do a fire drill and how to handle blood-borne pathogens.*

He grabs a few extra pens and some blank paper. If he plans it just right, he'll look extra studious "taking notes" when in fact he's filling out a Buzzword Bingo card.

He kisses his sleeping wife and walks into his daughter's bedroom, crushing his toes on the tiny sprawling disassembled Lego village. He nestles the teddy bear up against her face and for a moment, he's hopeful again.

Then he leaves. The drive is painfully slow. Every street is being torn-up and refurbished. Orange and white traffic barricades block him from moving where he wants to move. Like the tie and the title and the PowerPoint presentations, it's all the same symptom. Something is broken, really broken, but we don't know how to fix it, we will look busy and constantly re-invent and reconstruct and hope that we can convince people that novelty equals change.

"I'm tired of the barricades," he says aloud.

*I'm tired of the noise. I'm tired of the next best thing and the jargon and the well-intentioned gestures. I'm tired of the cage and the tie and the title and the staff handbook and the blood borne pathogen video. I'm tired of pretending to like people I don't*

*know and pretending to know people I don't like. I'm
tired. That's it. I'm just really, really tired.*

He turns up the radio louder this time. If he can
just focus on the monotonous tone of morning
public radio, maybe he'll hear a depressing story
about genocide and he'll be able to regain a solitary
sense of being thankful for the job.

Turns out it's just a pundit spouting out phrases
like "high standards" and "transparency" and
"accountability" to try and justify the newest
educational reforms. The pundit blames the lousy,
lazy teachers and their awful unions.

"I work hard. I put in crazy hours. It's just that
I'm tired, angry-pundit-man. I'm really tired. And
after a summer of curriculum planning and the
barrage of mandatory workshops I'm even more
tired than ever." The pundit doesn't listen. Nobody
listens. That's the hard part. Nobody ever listens.

It's not that teachers burn out. They just
disappear. They slowly turn invisible, existing
without ever being present. Then one day, they log
in their hours and they're gone.

## What Is Burnout?

Burnout isn't simply quitting the teaching
profession. I've met teachers who are walking

zombies, lacking any passion or purpose as they move through the drudgery of their job. They're not all veteran teachers, either. There are teachers who burn out in the first year and by the second year, they are already burnt out.

To me, burnout is when someone loses the essence of teaching - that purpose and passion and identity that allow a person to thrive. Burnout is why so many teachers fail to make it past the third year of teaching (though to be honest the crappy pay doesn't help). It's why certain teachers fast track their way into administrator and coaching roles (this isn't to suggest that administrators and coaches are simply burnt out teachers). But it's also why so many teachers get up in the morning dreading work.

| What Burnout Is | What Burnout Isn't |
|---|---|
| Losing your passion as a teacher | Losing some of your energy as a teacher |
| Dreading going to work every day | Having days when you just don't feel like being there (we all have those days) |
| Feeling empty | Feeling tired |
| Giving up as a teacher | Moving into a new role (as a principal, coach, etc.) |

Not all teachers who leave the profession are burnt out. Here in my home state of Arizona, I have met many teachers who left the profession because the pay was too low. That's not burnout. That's simply the dark reality of a population that refuses to fund public education. Teachers go into this profession to make a difference. However, it's hard to keep going when a teacher has to decide between paying for health care or groceries. See, I've met teachers who give up after working extra jobs as servers, bartenders, tutors or retail workers. That's not burnout. That's simply the result of not being able to make ends meet.

## Why Teachers Burn Out

People often assume burnout occurs because teachers work too hard, put in too many hours and don't take care of themselves. Just go to the gym, eat well and you'll be fine. Yet, few people ask *why* a teacher felt that she had to work so hard, put in so many extra hours and sacrifice a personal life.

My guess is that the root cause is perfectionism. There's an ideal picture of what a teacher should be and teachers will work at unhealthy levels to live up to this perfect image. Perfectionism is dangerous because it takes a shot at the identity, forcing a person to act better and try harder. Perfectionism takes a shot at the purpose of education, feeding teachers the lie that the goal is measurable results rather than faithfulness. It becomes a shaming message screaming at a teacher like a red-faced football coach, "Get up you pansy and try harder! Pull yourself up and prove it! Prove that you're better than this!"

I've never seen a teacher burn out from working too hard. However, I have seen teachers burn out from the relentless pursuit of perfection that often leads to insane work hours. I've seen teachers refuse to set boundaries because of the sense of martyrdom we're supposed to have. I've seen teachers get so knocked down with shame that they can hardly function professionally. I've seen teachers put up a façade of professionalism while they quietly suffer in isolation. Here are a few of the things that I have seen lead to teacher burnout:

1. *Unreasonable Expectations:* This is similar to perfectionism. However, it's more about what teachers expect externally from the job. Some teachers think things will work out when they just get rid of "that kid." Some teachers think that they will find the perfect school where the kids sit still and the rules all make sense and the

staff is filled with people who never gossip. This lingering disappointment can lead to burnout.

2.  *Micromanaging Leaders:* Losing autonomy can be crushing for some teachers. It can feel like walking on eggshells. Okay, not true. It's more like walking on a bed of nails. It sucks. Sometimes the issue is less about the leadership and more about the system. Either way, teachers reach a place where they lose their passion.

3.  *Negative School Culture:* It's hard to teach in a place where there is fear, hostility and backbiting. I've been pretty fortunate in the places where I've taught. However, I've seen teachers hit a point of burnout only to thrive in a new environment.

4.  *Shame:* Teachers who have been shamed for bad scores (either by the system or by administrators) end up wounded. It's not surprising when good teachers decide to pack it up and go home. However, sometimes it's much more personal. Perhaps it is a student comment, a parent complain, a wall of apathy, or a cruel rumor that pushes teachers into a place of numb indifference. Maybe it's a horrible moment as a teacher where they

screwed up and they still haven't forgiven themselves. In these moments, some teachers learn to hedge their bets emotionally so they won't get hurt again. In the process, they lose their passion.

5.  *Violating Your Beliefs:* The closest I've been to walking away have been the moments when I was asked to abandon real teaching for test prep. There have been moments when I looked at the six weeks a year of testing and wanted to walk away from it. I've seen great teachers leave the profession because they simply cannot work any longer in a system that can feel so soul crushing.

6.  *Ignoring Identity:* I know some things about myself. I can't be on too many committees or I get cynical. I don't do well in leadership, because I end up trying to please everyone and avoid conflict. I can't do loud, noisy spaces. Sometimes great teachers lose their passion, because they aren't teaching out of their identity.

7.  *Wrong Context:* In some cases, teachers burn out because they are in the wrong teaching context. While there is a danger in constantly searching for that "perfect class," there are

times when a teacher simply needs a different grade level or subject matter.

8. *Boredom:* This tends to be an issue with veteran teachers who reach a place where they plateau. Teaching gets boring. It's no longer challenging for them. Over time the boredom leads to slow, fading burnout.

9. *Isolation:* Although solitude and self-reflection are vital for teachers, they also need to connect to community. Teachers need trusted relationships where they are affirmed for who they are rather than what they accomplish. They need spaces where they can be vulnerable without worrying about being judged.

10. *People Pleasing:* Too often, I have defined success by whether or not parents, administrators, colleagues or students were happy with me. I started to care about test scores. I joined committees and took on responsibilities because I thought it would make someone happy. Over time, this drive to keep others happy gets exhausting and the only option left is walking away.

11. *Unicorns:* Oh, sure, you think they're cute and whatnot. But they're basically magical horses with swords on their heads. Never seen a

unicorn? It's probably because no one has ever lived to see one. But I'm telling you, a run-in with unicorns can be a real career killer.

I've seen great teachers leave the profession entirely. It was often a combination of the factors mentioned above. In most cases, they weren't able to articulate why the burnout was occurring and they didn't start taking steps to change things until it was too late.

What if we took a more proactive approach? What if we thought ahead of time about fireproofing our profession so that we didn't have great teachers leaving in droves?

## The Approach:

These are meant to be strategies rather than solutions. They are flexible concepts that you can make your own. We're all on a journey (myself included). I start this book out with identity and the story a teacher chooses. From there I move to your ultimate goal and your definition of success. Although there are practical ideas within this book, I ultimately believe that the mindset, beliefs, story and approach to teaching matter far more than the steps or keys or whatever else.

# The Spark
# Within

\* \* \*

*Strategy #1:*
*Teach out of your identity.*

Every summer I have nightmares. Sometimes the dreams are odd - like the one where our school became a charter school owned by terrorists and I was charged with defending my classroom using only a balloon animal sword. Usually, though, it's a giant unfurnished classroom. The walls are empty and I step in completely unprepared. Nothing I do works. Sometimes I stammer out instructions or cannot get the words to come out of my mouth. Other times I rant and rave and yell at the students.

One year, I lived that nightmare. It shook me to my core. I had decided to move down to sixth grade self-contained and it bombed completely. None of the preventative discipline I knew worked. The lessons tanked. The students didn't respond well to me. I yelled. It wasn't as bad as the nightmares I had experienced but it was still bad. After all, our school was never taken over by terrorists. Still, by December, I wanted to quit. Then things turned around . . . slightly. Going to work was still a challenge. Lessons never worked quite the way they were supposed to. I still had to work at classroom management (something that hadn't been an issue in years).

I remember talking to my best friend Javi about the situation.

"I think I'm burned out," I told him.

"No you're not. You're just tired," he said.

"But I don't look forward to going to work anymore."

"Of course you don't. It's really hard. It's the hardest year you've ever had. But it taught you something you never completely realized before."

I shook my head.

"It taught you that you are a teacher. And it taught you that you can handle anything. But it also taught you something else: just because you *can* handle that kind of year doesn't mean you *should* have that kind of year again."

Javi was right. The sheer fact that I made it so far was proof that I was a teacher. Growth had been slow but I had still improved. Even in a difficult year, I had proven that I was a teacher.

However, I also knew that I couldn't teach like that forever. I had been spending all year teaching in a way that didn't fit my identity. Along the way, I learned a few things about myself:

- Autonomy matters to me. I can't teach in a role where we are planning all of our lessons together because I can't teach someone else's lessons. There's nothing wrong with collaboration. However, I need space to create my own projects with my students.
- I can't live in fear of low test scores. I work best when I am able to define success with a more meaningful metric. If I am teaching to the test, I am ultimately teaching in a way that goes against everything I believe about education.
- I work best in a departmentalized format, where I have a different group of kids every class period. I

like the chance to teach a similar lesson to different groups so that I can refine my craft and reflect on my practices as I'm teaching.

- I need to be able to teach in a project-based format. I don't do well when I am stuck in a method that is too traditional for me.
- I'm an introvert. I need to have spaces that are a little quieter. I need to have prep period where I sit alone and plan. I need to have the permission to eat my lunch by myself instead of going to the staff lounge.

I realized, at this point, that I needed to switch to a different context. After spending a year teaching out of my weaknesses, I had to find a position that fit my strengths. So, I moved to a seventh and eighth grade photojournalism and computer position where I am thriving. I had to move into a place where I had more autonomy and creativity. I needed to be in a place where the context fit my identity.

## Teaching Out of Your Identity

Teaching begins internally. It starts with that spark that leads you into the profession. The beliefs you hold, the values you have, the sense of purpose – these all begin somewhere deep within you. This is why identity is so important. When you are teaching in a way that doesn't fit your identity, you are unable to teach to your full potential. You are more likely to angry and irritable. There's a constant feeling that something isn't right.

On the other hand, when you are teaching out of your identity, things work harmoniously. You feel more energized. You feel more content. You are able to teach out of your strengths. You have a certain level of control over how you are doing. It's not hard for you to see the sense of purpose in your daily routine. In many cases, it feels more enjoyable.

Too often, teachers ignore identity. They spend their time teaching out of what others *expect* them to be rather than who they *need* to be. They ignore the spark inside of them. It gets tiring first, then exhausting and then eventually it leads to burnout.

## Am I Cut Out to Be a Teacher?

You might be sitting there wondering if maybe you are fit to be a teacher. You may be wondering if maybe teaching doesn't fit your identity. I can't answer that for you. The truth is that there are some teachers who aren't cut out for the profession. I've known people who despised the age group that they taught. I've met folks who had no interest in their subject matter. Although I think these teachers are rare, they exist and they are toxic to learning.

Think about why you became a teacher. Forget about the time you've invested in the program, the diploma you earned or the people you've talked to about your plans. Think about your identity for a moment.

*Are you a teacher?*
*Are you passionate about learning?*
*Do you care deeply about children in your classroom?*

If you answered, "no" to these questions, leave now. Cut your losses on your degree and save yourself the pain that you will experience on a daily basis. It will be like leaving a bad relationship. You'll be humbled, but you'll be relieved. Chances are you'll make more money doing something else.

If you can answer, "yes," to all three questions, you're a teacher. If you are a teacher, hold onto this identity as closely as you possibly can. There will be times you question yourself. Maybe you suck at paperwork. Maybe you get too angry about standardized tests. You'll see teachers who are naturally peppy and you'll wonder if you're too cynical.

Other times, it will be internal. You'll fail badly. You'll yell at kids. If you are willing to own your journey, you won't blame the kids and you'll be stuck with the reality of your own imperfection. In darker moments, you'll question whether or not the students would be better off with a different teacher. You'll get tired and wonder if the whole teaching gig is worth it. You'll see a lack of progress and if you're not careful, you'll buy into the lie that there's a quick-fix solution that you somehow haven't figured out.

But if your answer was "yes" to those three questions, then the spark is inside of you. And for that reason alone, you will be able to grow. If you remember that you are a teacher, that it is a part of your identity, then you will be more likely to teach out of who you are. If you can do that, you can thrive. You can be yourself. You can work out of your strengths. And, in the long run, you can avoid burnout.

## Reflection Questions

- What are your strengths? To what extent does your current position play to those strengths?
- What are your weaknesses? To what extent are you having to teach out of your weaknesses? (i.e.

having a hard time with the cynicism of junior high or the energy level of second graders)

- Are you more introverted or extroverted? Do you feel energized by what you are doing or exhausted? Does your current position allow you the right amount of time with other people?
- Do you thrive on autonomy or do you crave collaboration? How does this compare to your current position?
- Is there a particular subject that you are passionate about? Are you getting enough of a chance to teach that subject?
- Are you better off with the variety of multiple subjects or do you prefer to teach the same thing multiple times and refine your lessons?
- Do you thrive in a place of noise and chaos or are you better off when there is silence and order?

## Action Ideas

Take a strength and weakness inventory as a teacher. This allows you to look honestly and who you are and what that means, in terms of your approach to teaching. While it might not seem practical at first, this exercise can be powerful as a way to frame what you will do in the classroom.

The following chart can be helpful as you figure it out:

| Strengths: What are your strengths as a teacher? | Weaknesses: What are your weaknesses as a teacher? |
|---|---|
| Opportunities: What opportunities do you have as a result of your strengths? | Threats: What are some of the things that threaten your success as a teacher? What can you do protect yourself in your weaknesses? |

The following chart can be helpful as you figure out how your identity connects to your approach to teaching:

| Identity | Pros | Cons | Next steps |
|----------|------|------|------------|
|          |      |      |            |
|          |      |      |            |
|          |      |      |            |

# Fireworks
# or Fire Works?

\* \* \*

### Strategy #2:
### Choose a better story.

I'm lousy at trying to start a fire. Blame it on the fact that I never joined Boy Scouts or maybe the fact that "camping" when I was a kid involved hanging out in an RV. Whatever the reason, I always screw up a campfire. I begin too big, with large logs and lots of smoke. Sometimes I cheat by trying to douse the wood with lighter fluid. My wife, however, has it all figured out. It begins with smaller wood, some starter sticks and a little flame. There's always room to let the fire breathe. After awhile, the fire grows until, without realizing it, we have something warm and powerful and capable of turning an ordinary marshmallow into something magical.

I'm not exactly sure how fire works, but it seems to be the opposite approach to fireworks. Fireworks are more entertaining - huge explosive displays of color, ear-splitting booms, the murmuring of "oohs" and "ahhs." Light a fuse and watch the explosion. It's instant and impressive.

I was thinking about this the other night while sitting in front of a fire pit. I was thinking about teacher movies. Each movie seemed to glorify the firework approach to teaching. The main character ascends to the furthest reaches of the sky and passionately explodes with huge results. All of a sudden students of poverty are doing calculus and falling in love with literature.

The Silverscreen Superteachers are impressive. They're loud and colorful and entertaining. Yet, like fireworks, the teachers featured in the movies only lasted a few years. I couldn't think of a single "based on a true story" movie where the true story didn't lead to the teacher leaving after less than a decade in the classroom. If teaching is a marathon, these movies were short snippets of wind sprints. They were supposed to be inspirational but the only thing they could inspire was a story of burnout.

I want to be a teacher with a steady passion that lasts a career. Instead of a loud, thundering message and a flashy display of lights, I want to be a steady fire that can maintain a small community and provide a platform for dialogue. The best campfires aren't the center of attention. Instead, they serve as a place of warmth where others can grow close together. I want that to be my approach as a teacher – humble and focused on the classroom community.

By contrast, a firework show might be more entertaining. It'll pack a stadium full of spectators. However, the truth is that it's an endless, loud, amazing display of burnout. I don't want that to be my story as a teacher.

## The Wrong Story

Stories are a powerful way to make sense out of our lives. As I think about my career as a teacher, I find that there are two types of stories I can choose. One is the firework story and the other is the campfire story.

| | Fireworks | Campfire |
|---|---|---|

| Protagonist | I want to be successful in quantitative, bold, measurable terms. I want to be known as successful. | I want to be faithful, wise and humble. I want to be someone who loved people well. |
|---|---|---|
| Antagonist | Lazy teachers and lazy students | Standardized education and the lie of perfection |
| Plot | An amazing Hollywood-style story, something newsworthy and amazing | A small story filled with little daily things that make a difference over time |
| Conflict | Will I save the world? Will I make a difference? | Will I remain true to my convictions? Will I react in humility? |
| Theme | Make a difference | Be faithful and serve |

## Chasing Fireworks

I began my teaching career because I saw the job as meaningful. I wanted to do something that mattered. However, in my first year, after seeing movies like *Stand and Deliver,* I felt inspired to be a Superman swooping into the city and saving the day. I went from wanting to serve to wanting to make a difference. A big difference. The kind of difference that people would make people marvel.

Armed with handful of Hollywood prototypes, I now had a new story which involved both being perfect and expecting perfection from my students. I saw the antagonist as the other teachers who were pushing "low standards." My theme had moved from faithfulness to making a difference and being noticed.

Outwardly, this approach looked successful. Students were working hard and reading more challenging literature. We were filming a documentary. I had a philosophy club meeting each morning before school. However, I felt hollow. I became sarcastic toward students, because I expected perfection. I grew overly critical of myself until eventually I grew critical of students. I felt like they owed me something. I snapped at students over the smallest mistakes. I was a disaster of a teacher. I found the following things to be the result of the fireworks approach:

- Perfectionism: I work harder to live up to an unreasonable expectation of myself. I yelled at a student, so now I'll be an overly optimistic Mr. Rogers (for what it's worth, I bet I could rock a cardigan). I forget to turn in some paperwork, so now I'll become a hyper-organized professional.

- Unreasonable Student Expectations: I start to believe that if I am working really hard to prove myself, my students need to respond in kind. I view it as a social contract where they owe me the same work that I put in.

- No Sense of Humor: I quit laughing. I quit smiling. I convince myself that there is no longer a place for joking in a profession where the stakes are so high.

- Isolation: I no longer work with others, because I am trying to solve things on my own and prove to others that I am not weak. Moreover, without showing any signs of weakness, nobody knows that I am in such an ugly place, so they generally leave me alone. This fuels the sense of self-doubt about who I am as a teacher.

- Misinterpretation: I start to see events without a hint of realism. A student misbehaves and I respond with the assumption that it's a personal attack on my character, when, in fact, that student is actually very social and simply wants to talk.

- Lack of Trust: I quit trusting myself, my students and my colleagues. I feel like I have to prove that

I don't need any help. To be honest, there's no way they can trust me when I'm wearing the superhero mask, because they don't even get a chance at seeing the real me.

- Anger: I get angry when others fail to perform up to my high standards and I get even angrier when I fail.
- Risk Aversion: I become overly guarded in my approach, trying my best to avoid mistakes, because I haven't give myself permission to fail.
- Resignation: I give up. I teach without energy. I lose my passion.

That last one is what ultimately leads to burnout. After exploding in perfectionism, I am nothing more than a shell of a teacher, burnt out and falling from the sky. The good news is I can change course and opt for the campfire story. I can focus on being faithful. I can humble myself as a teacher. I can define success by standards that matter rather than focusing on test scores. I can remember that students don't need rock stars. They need compassionate adults who are dedicated to honing their craft as teachers.

## The Power of Smaller Stories

## THE FIREPROOF TEACHER

I've had moments when I have been really critical about my older son's experience in school. I've been bold about his experiences with homework or behavior charts or multiple-choice tests. And yet . . . he loves his class. He still loves his teacher. He still loves learning. He's being challenged to think more deeply. He's learning the honest reality of history. When I talk to him, I am reminded that teachers can be "wrong" about certain things and still get it so right.

For every time he tells me about a frustrating math packet, there are ten times he tells me about something funny she said or a time he learned something cool or a moment she encouraged him in a way that affirmed who he is as a person.

Last night my son read aloud three short stories he had written. I watched him get into the zone as he focused on the fourth. As I stepped back and watched it, I felt grateful for his teacher. I knew the hours it took for her to edit the work. I knew the lessons she had to teach to get him to develop better word choice and sentence fluency. It has me thinking that there are a lot of little stories (the kind that don't end up on keynote slides or blog posts) that still add up to something powerful. He loves writing due in large part to his teacher.

I mention this because I regret the times in the past when I posted my frustration about my son's homework. I regret the fact that I only told the critical stories. I regret the tone of superiority that I took. Because here's the thing: my kid can read. I have no idea how phonics and blending and all of that work. But he can read. My son is learning two-step equations and he's learning it in a conceptual way that is so much better than the way I learned it. I didn't teach him those things. His teacher did.

It has me thinking that there are amazing, epic things that are happening in schools and too often we fail to notice them because they are so common. They are campfire stories of small success – tiny fires that grow and turn into a bold, lasting flame. Sometimes we miss these small successes because we believe that the goal is something big and grand and colorful and loud.

I wonder if telling more of these smaller stories would ultimately prevent teachers from burning out. The truth is that amazing things are happening but because they are small or even common, we start to think they are ordinary or even insignificant. It has me thinking that by telling these stories and thanking teachers for their role in these stories, we might be able to help prevent burnout.

## Reflection Questions

1. Do you agree with the premise that a humble, quieter, smaller story is more effective in preventing teacher burnout?
2. What kind of story do you find yourself believing? Why? Where does that come from?
3. Where does the lie of perfectionism come from? How can we change that?
4. In what moments are you most tempted to shift toward a fireworks approach?
5. What is a time when you bought in to the wrong kind of story as a teacher?

## Action Ideas

Think through your current story as a teacher. Go through the Elements of Literature with the following questions.

- Setting: Where are you? What do you believe about the place where you teach?
- Plot: How would you describe your plot? What small victories should you celebrate?
- Conflict: What is the ultimate goal? What is success? How do you define it?
- Antagonist: Are you blaming the system or blaming people?

Before taking on a huge project ask yourself why you are doing it? Is it to get noticed? Is it to prove something to someone? Or is it because you are doing something that matters?

Make an effort to find small things that are pretty awesome in your own building. Send a thank you note or an email to that staff member affirming that teacher in what he or she is accomplishing.

# A Slow and Steady Burn

* * *

**Strategy #3:**
**Define success as faithfulness and growth**
**rather than results or perfection.**

In the previous chapter, I mentioned the two stories that you can choose as a teacher. Ultimately, those two stories shape how we define success. Do you choose faithfulness or perfection? Do you see mistakes as a part of growth or as evidence that we suck as teachers? These stories ultimately drive what you believe about success, which ultimately prevents burnout.

## When I Failed

I knew there was an issue when the test asked students to choose which resource they would most likely use in research. The options were something like: atlas, dictionary, textbook, and almanac. (Heads-up: I'm modifying this just so I don't get accused of sharing test questions.) In my class, the answer was "none of the above." We used Google. We used social media. We sought out experts from around the globe.

There was another question asking the theme of a book called *Broncos, Bucks and Spurs.* None of my students chose "life on the range." They all chose sports, because those were the names of sports franchises (although it's debatable whether or not the Milwaukee Bucks are really playing like a true NBA franchise right now).

Initially, I shrugged it off. The kids screwed up on a quarterly benchmark. They would be fine in the long run. However, I began to feel sick to my stomach as I saw just how low the scores actually were. Suddenly, I was *that* teacher. I was the one with some of the lowest scores in the district.

I received an email the next morning telling me that I needed to send a list of "bubble kids." You might be picturing John Travolta in *Boy in the*

*Bubble,* but really they were asking for the kids who were close to passing but somehow missed the cut. That was actually most of my class. None of them did as well as they were supposed to do. A minute later, I received an email asking me if I needed a coach to come in and help me with my reading lessons. Suddenly emails flooded in asking if I wanted "guidance" or "support." I had gone from a model classroom that struggling teachers would observe to being the teacher who needed help.

There was a scarlet letter. Or perhaps more accurately, there was a scarlet number for the entire district to see. It was a data point shouting out, "Spencer sucks!" Suddenly coaches offered help. Fellow teachers offered resources.

I don't mind learning from failure, but this was a different kind of failure, because I had such little control over the metrics. It was shaming. And the problem with shame is that you don't learn from it. You recover from it.

I remember driving home thinking, *Am I still a good teacher?* I was ready to send an email offering my resignation. I wanted to tell myself that the scores didn't matter but I couldn't convince myself to shrug it off.

It took me weeks to recover. It's amazing how the emotions lingered even after the mindset readjusted. Slowly, though, I was able to realize that I had been defining success in all the wrong ways.

I had defined success based upon whether or not it made someone else happy (in this case my district). This moment helped me realize that I had to define success on my terms, based upon my personal satisfaction of a job well done. More importantly, I realized that I needed to define success based upon whether or not my students were learning.

I had defined success on the wrong kind of metric. I didn't even believe in standardized tests. Yet I allowed test scores to be my bottom line. In the process, I had defined success based upon something totally outside of my control. I realized, in that moment, that I could not control whether a test was good or bad. I could not control how my students would react to a bad test. What I could control were the things like the instruction, the assessment and the culture of my classroom.

The end result was that I had defined success out of fear. I was afraid of being seen as a bad teacher. I was afraid of the school going into school improvement. I was afraid of disappointing my fellow teachers. I was afraid of getting fired (highly unlikely based upon one quarter of lower scores). I had never even considered whether or not these fears were unfounded. I had simply bought into the fear and allowed it to define my view of success.

## A Slow Burning Fire

Part of my problem is that I had bought into a fireworks definition of success. After being recognized and noticed as a teacher, I had believed the lie that the test scores mattered. The problem with that standard is that it ultimately could only lead to arrogance when I succeeded and shame when I failed. And I had gotten really arrogant. When we define success through a fireworks story, the end results are often:

- An External Focus: We begin to forget about motives and pay more attention to results. This can lead to burnout because teachers end up trusting something totally outside their control to define whether or not they are doing well.
- A Lack of Self-Reflection: When success is all about the end result, we lose sight on the process. We quit self-reflecting.
- Comparing to Others: Like a firework exploding above the crowd, we feel a need to

prove that we are better than others. This leads to distrust of peers. It breeds arrogance when we succeed and shame when we fail.

Here's where the campfire mindset matters. It's a slow and steady burn. It's about faithfulness rather than perfection. It's about student learning rather than student test scores. It's about serving humbly rather than being recognized as an amazing teacher. It's about growing and improving rather than attaining a flawless perfection.

Here, teachers define success by whether or not they have grown rather than whether or not they have achieved a goal. Instead of living in fear of failure, they realize that screwing up is ultimately a chance to learn. It's a chance to figure out what to do differently and to improve as a result. The campfire mindset also allows teachers to see growth as incremental. The fact that it is slow doesn't mean it's not happening. Because it's not external, teachers are then more likely to reach out to others because it's not a competition.

This is a sharp contrast to much of the rhetoric we hear about teaching. "Never settle for second best," they say. We toss around words like, "success at all costs" and "achieve more" and implore people to work harder when it's not perfect. However, when I see effective teachers who have lasted decades in this profession, they seem content. They seem to take mistakes in stride and continue to grow as a result. They aren't under the illusion that they will reach perfection – or even the idea that perfection is something they should strive for.

In most cases, they define success internally. They take ownership of their craft and realize that they cannot easily change the context of education. There is a rugged realism to the slow steady burn of the campfire story. These teachers know how to keep the fire going because success is always about growth. It's always about keeping the fire going no matter what kind of storm rages around them.

| Campfire | Fireworks |
|---|---|
| Being faithful | Measurable Success |
| Internally-driven | Externally-driven |
| Healthy risks | Risk-aversion |
| Growth is incremental with ups and downs | Growth is instant and constant |
| Community is vital for thriving | Community is a threat |
| Cooperation is key | Competition is key |

## Remembering What Matters

Sometimes I get into this place as a teacher where I look back at my former years and shake my head. I get critical about how traditional I was or how I picked battles over homework. I think of every incident where I was critical or angry. I cringe at the times I yelled at a class.

Over the last few months, though, I've gotten Facebook friend requests from former students. Suddenly I'm wishing them the best on being moms and dads or husbands or wives. I'm talking them through a small crisis in college. Inevitably I end up saying something like, "I'm sorry for how I handled _____" and the response is nearly always the same.

They've forgotten.

What they remember, though, is the goofy accents I used or the jokes I told. They remember a particular project we did together that I have already forgotten. They remember that one conversation where I had the chance to encourage a student at a time of need. They nearly always circle back to two things: what they learned and the fact that I cared. Despite all my imperfections, that's what they remember.

If I've nailed those two things, I'm doing okay. I will continue to grow. I will continue to learn. I will continue to screw up and say that I'm sorry. But the truth remains that what really matters are the same two things that have always mattered. Do I care about my students? Are they learning?

I ran into a student the other day. She had a slip of paper with feedback I had scribbled out on the side. At first I cringed at the word Bell Work and the rigid format I had once required.

"You kept your Bell Work?" I asked.

She shook her head. "Just read it, Mr. Spencer."

It was an assignment about the barriers she had faced in her education. She mentioned a dad who called her stupid all the time. The fact that she didn't have documentation as an immigrant meant she felt like she had no future. She mentioned school being hard for her.

On the side, I had written, "You're intelligent. You're a brilliant writer and a deep thinker. You'll go places in life."

"I kept that through high school and I've kept it through college. I hope that doesn't sound weird."

"It doesn't," I told her.

"Anyway, I just thought you should know that those words encouraged me. It was a reminder that words have power and, um, yeah, thanks for believing in me before I could believe in myself."

These moments are rare. They happen once every year or two. However, they are a reminder that despite all the times I have screwed up as a teacher, the ultimate measure of success remains the same. Do I care about my students? Are they learning? If I can keep that as my definition of success, I'm not going to burn out.

## Reflection Questions

The following questions can be helpful in making sense out of how we define success. Take a look at them and self-reflect on your story as a teacher and how you choose to define success:

1. What is your ultimate goal?
2. What does success look like? How will you know when you have achieved it?
3. Who is defining the standard of success that you are setting?
4. How much control do you have in whether or not you are successful based upon that standard?
5. What happens if you fail to meet that standard of success? How do you respond? What are your next steps?

## Action Ideas

- Watch any of the teacher movies with a group of fellow teachers and lead a discussion on the story. The following questions might be helpful:
  - o How does this movie square with your reality as a teacher?
  - o What part of the story does Hollywood omit?
  - o What are some of the actions the protagonist is doing that might ultimately lead to burnout?
  - o How are they defining success in this movie? How does this compare and contrast to your own definition of success?
- Read Carol Dweck's *Mindset.* There are some many relevant ideas connected to the concept of growth, mistakes, and how we define success.
- Be open to the fact that you will always need to grow as a teacher. Some of the best feedback you can get is from students. I start with a student evaluation form and then I set professional goals and a plan of action. You can access all of this in the free Professional Growth Framework.

# Don't Let the Fire Consume You

* * *

**Strategy #4:**
**Set boundaries and stick to them.**

I don't believe that hard work causes teacher burnout. I don't believe that a teacher who works sixty hours a week will automatically crash and burn. I know of a teacher who is still teaching at sixty-two and she works close to seventy hours a week. It works for her, because she spends most of that time doing things that energize her. She works in a school garden and takes care of the creatures in her classroom. She counsels with kids and helps them navigate college acceptance. She's amazing.

However, I can't be that kind of teacher. Between being a dad and a husband, I can't leave at six in the morning and be home at seven at night. I need space to think and write. I need to be away from people. I've been there before – in that crazy, hectic, frantic pace. I threw myself into teaching out of a sense of obligation and duty. I believed the best teachers were martyrs, which is kind of dumb because self-imposed martyrdom is essentially voluntary burnout.

Things have changed since then. I don't allow the fire to consume me. I work less. I set boundaries. I pursue projects outside of my classroom that fuel my fire. Ultimately, these are all a part of why I haven't burned out.

## Working Forty Hours a Week

I was excited about going back to school on the Monday after Winter Break. I know, I know. This flies in the face of all the Facebook posts and memes about wanting just one more day of vacation. However, I was ready to be back. I had planned a coding project with one group, a blogging project with another and a multimedia package project with the third. I couldn't wait to see what my students would create. This excitement was the byproduct of my passion for teaching.

In the past, the passion I had for teaching meant I also felt compelled to work harder and spend more hours on classroom-related activities. I had to grade every paper, because that's what kids deserved. I had to join every committee because I felt like a Constructivist perspective was needed. I coached sports because it was important for me to know the kids relationally. When I wasn't coaching, I was attending games because I needed them to know that I cared. We did service learning projects on the weekend and spent late hours on Friday nights painting murals.

But it was more than that. It wasn't just about the students. I wanted to prove to teachers that I was a great teacher. I heard about "those teachers" who showed up right before contract time and left right when it ended. "Those teachers" were the burnouts. They were the babysitters. They were the ones just phoning it in.

I'm now one of those teachers. I show up at 7:30 a.m. and leave at 4:00 p.m. If I substitute my thirty-minute lunch, I am working forty hours a week. True, I lesson plan and create resources over the summer, but it's mostly because I find that stuff to be fun. The reality is I am not overworked. I am not constantly stressed out. And I'm not sorry about this.

I love being a teacher, but I also love being a dad and a husband. I love writing books. I love blogging. I love reading. I love binge-watching *Sherlock*. I'm still passionate about my job. I still care about students. None of that has changed as I have slowly dropped down to a forty-hour-a-week schedule. When I mention this to people, there is an assumption that I must be cutting corners. However, I have found that these certain strategies have allowed me to work within a schedule:

- Using prep time for real prep. I don't use that time to go to the staff lounge. I don't stop by the vending machines. I spend this time filling out rubrics, leaving comments on student work, and planning lessons.
- Dealing with discipline issues relationally. It's amazing how much time I save by not writing referrals and detention slips. If a student acts up in class, we talk about it in the moment. It's a relational, conversational approach that works -- but also one that means less time chasing kids down and managing a system.
- Grading less but assessing more. My grade book consists of the standards and the mastery

toward each one. I use constant formative assessment so that I can figure out what each student is earning. I couple this with the project rubrics. This means I'm not filling the grade book with hundreds of assignments. I'm not spending my time on data entry.

- Assessing during class. If I'm walking around seeing how students are doing, I might as well use that time to add comments to student blogs or pull kids aside for one-on-one conferencing.

- Cutting out the fluff. For example, I don't decorate my class. I leave that to the students. Something as small as that can make a huge difference in terms of time.

- Working during the summer. I know this isn't really a "time saver" per se. However, I make all my unit plans and lesson materials over the summer. This then allows me to focus on lesson planning and grading during the school year.

I've always said, "I want to teach so that I can help kids think well about life," but I spent the first five years of teaching allowing teaching to be my entire life. I claimed to believe in living well but I didn't have a life outside of school. That's not true anymore. I work around forty hours a week and I love what I'm doing but I also have a vibrant life outside of school.

## Setting Boundaries

Somewhere in my fourth or fifth year of teaching, my wife pulled me aside and said, "We will get you back at some point." It was a gentle nudge, but the words echoed through my mind for an entire weekend. Between getting a master's degree and throwing myself into school projects, I was completely exhausted when I was home.

I didn't want to be that kind of dad. I didn't want to be that kind of husband, either. I began to set boundaries so that teaching wouldn't consume me. Here are some things that were helpful for me:

- Set a firm boundary of when work stops and starts. I made it a rule that I would be home at 5:30 pm everyday. Now, it's gotten closer to 4:30 pm or 5:00 pm.
- Grade at work. I don't take stacks of papers home to grade on the weekends.
- Don't take work home mentally, either. People are quick to criticize compartmentalization, but here's a reality: If I'm playing catch with my kids in the backyard, they deserve my full attention in that moment. I shouldn't be

planning lessons in my mind when I'm interacting with them.

- Say no to things that don't directly impact your students and don't fuel your fire as a teacher. I'm not a member of the Sunshine Committee. I don't chaperone dances. I don't coach sports anymore. Some people are energized by those things. However, they wear me out.
- Outsource whatever you can to the students.
- Get an organizational system down and stay on task while you are at work. Sometimes teachers work crazy hours because they're just not that efficient with the time that they have.
  - Communicate your boundaries with someone you care about. Allow that person to remind you of the boundaries you have created.

The truth is that we are in a helping profession. Most of us went into this gig because we wanted to make a difference. The unhealthy side of this is that many teachers can get so consumed by the profession that the profession consumes them. There will always be work to do and not enough time to do it.

However, by setting boundaries, teachers get the work that needs to be done accomplished and spend their free time doing things that fuel their fire away in the classroom.

## Teaching Isn't My Life Anymore

After setting firm boundaries, I began to get my life back. Right now, teaching isn't the top priority in my life. That might sound harsh, but it's true. I love teaching. I'm passionate about what I do. However, it isn't the sole focus of my world. See, when teaching was my single passion, I threw myself into the fire and had nothing left to give. I missed out of on my family. I missed out on creative endeavors. I lost myself in my role as a teacher and I was never able to step out of that. In other words, instead of teaching out of my identity, I allowed teaching to become my identity.

But now, years later, I'm having more fun teaching than ever before. I used to blog constantly and engaging in a bunch of Twitter chats because I felt the need to eat, sleep and breathe education. I'd feel shamed when my class didn't look like a utopia. So, I'd work harder, striving after perfection and never quite getting there. I guess I was going after the firework story. But now that teaching is less important, I can relax a little. I can have fun. I can go home and truly be at home.

I used to ask myself, "How can I keep this up for another thirty years?" The answer is simple. I couldn't keep it up. I didn't keep it up. However, now that teaching isn't the solitary focus consuming my life, the question is different. I now ask, "How would I possibly want to quit in thirty years?"

## Pursue a Hobby

After setting boundaries, I slowly had more time left in the day. I began drawing more and working on fiction. My wife and I published our first children's book, *Wendell the World's Worst Wizard.* I began working with a friend on developing a digital publishing platform for students. I carved out an autonomous space where I knew I could have blast. So even when teaching got tough, I had this other space in my world where I could thrive.

I find it odd that we tell students to be lifelong learners and pursue their passions and then far too often we allow the profession to get in the way of our own lifelong learning. Students deserve whole people who are actively learning and creating outside of the domain of the classroom. When we pursue a meaningful hobby, we're actually setting an example for our students. We are acting on the same advice that we give to kids.

I realize that this isn't easy. There is so much residual guilt attached to working less and setting boundaries. Sometimes other teachers get jealous. There are times when you will be viewed as less passionate or less dedicated or even lazy. Sometimes you'll even feel guilty about it. However, in the long run, you will maintain a steady fire rather than allowing the fire to consume you.

## Reflection Questions

1. How good are you at saying "no?" How do you respond when someone asks you to do something and you simply don't have time for it?

2. If you are working crazy hours out of obligation rather than passion, what types of fears might be fueling this?

3. How much of your time are you spending doing things that fit your passions, desires and identity?

4. What role does time management and organization play in your ability to set boundaries?

5. What kind of boundaries do you need to set?

## Action Ideas

- Learn to say no to things that simply do not matter.
- Set aside one evening a week as your own personal Genius Hour.
- Create your own set of boundaries. List what things you are willing and not willing to do. Place your list next to your school computer and review it weekly. In some cases, you might want to ask a trusted friend to keep you accountable.
- Do a time inventory. Track your time throughout an entire week. Take note of areas where you might be wasting time. You can access the free time inventory in the free resource *Teach More and Work Less.*
- Get organized. Think through your entire organizational system. The key thing is that you find a system that works for you. If you need practical ideas on how to get organized, you might want to check out *The Teacher's Guide to Getting Crap Done.*

# Focus on What Fuels the Flames

* * *

## Strategy #5:
## Be Realistic But Be Grateful

A few years back, I stumbled across a show about the "dirtiest jobs" in America. It struck me as I watched the show that most of the people who worked these jobs seemed to find satisfaction in their work. It was nothing sentimental. Nobody said, "I'm just really passionate about sorting through stinky garbage." However, the workers seemed to take pride in the fact that their work was literally saving lives.

In fact, as the host interviewed each employee, they mentioned work injuries and hard experiences, but each admitted that they had worked for nearly thirty years.

It has me thinking about teaching. The truth is that secretly I do so many things as a teacher for the recognition, for the enjoyment and for the sense of superiority I can feel when I have done something "big." However, ultimately, if I want to make it long-term as a teacher, I have to remember that this is a humbling job. It is often thankless.

Perhaps the good life is found in doing something that is meaningful on a daily basis even if it is thankless.

Recognizing teaching as a "dirty job" doesn't mean that I should deny or expect injustice. I will always speak out against the dark side of our testing culture. I will speak out against racism when I see it in our schools. I will be critical of things like bad homework or ridiculous packets. It also doesn't mean teachers should have to be martyrs. We should have a living wage and affordable healthcare. We should get adequate breaks that allow us to get rest. In some contexts, "do this for the children" becomes an excuse for teachers to act as doormats.

However, I never want to get into a mindset where I am constantly negative about teaching. Oddly enough, thinking of it as a potentially "dirty job" allows me to find enjoyment in all the great things I see. The truth is that we get to make a difference on a daily basis. We get to be creative in what we do. We get to have a job that provides some level of autonomy. We get to work a job that is challenging. Those things are ultimately what fuel our desire to stay within the profession.

A "dirty jobs" mindset is more about what we expect from the teaching profession. If we see it as inherently messy and challenging, we are more likely to make it in the long run. This mindset becomes the fuel that keeps a steady fire going for an entire career.

## Realistic Expectations

I have seen many teachers lose the fire because they had unrealistic expectations of the teaching profession. They made statements like, "If I just had a better class" or even "if that one kid would just move to another school." They were perpetually disappointed that teaching wasn't perfect.

Having realistic expectations starts with having a realistic view of humanity. I believe that people are both beautiful and broken. Bear with me for a second, but I'm going to bust out an old school metaphor. Think of it as a stained glass window. Modern science alone provides a wiry, cold, metallic view of humanity. It's not inaccurate per se, but it's empty. Thus, love or joy or sincerity can be reduced to firing ions and chemical reactions and muscular movements. On the other hand, art provides a tone and pulse and color that science misses. Yet, left on its own, it turns abstract and narcissistic. Blend the two together and you get the mystery of humanity, a stained glass window, cold and wiry and yet filled with color and tones. Now take that window and chuck a stone at it. That's us. Stained glass windows. Fragile and yet strong, beautiful and yet broken. Our stories are incomplete because of some pain, some shame, some event that shattered us.

When we hold onto this perspective, we are able to remain grateful. We expect the world to be broken but we know that beauty is possible. We are not shocked that teaching is a "dirty job" because we know that we are dealing with shards of glass and that sometimes it means you get hurt along the way. And yet, we can also see the good that exists in this world. This has long-term implications for how we approach teaching:

- I won't be shocked when a "good kid" does something bad or when a "bad kid" does something good because I will not keep a list of "good" and "bad" kids.
- I will forgive students and staff members when they screw up. I will also forgive myself when I screw up.
- I will never chase after the perfect system. I won't obsess over whether or not it is broken, because I know the world is broken. However, knowing that beauty exists, I will still work toward change. I will still look for ways to make life better for students.
- I can make a difference but you cannot change a child's world. There are factors that will break your heart and you will be helpless to try and fix this.

## The Power of Contentment

In education circles, we often hear phrases like "reach for the top" and "never settle for second best." We hear about innovation and pushing the envelope and being disruptive. There is a certain image of a leader as someone who is constantly shaking things up.

And yet . . .

When I see the best teachers in my building, I notice an often-overlooked trait. They are content. They are satisfied with the work they are doing. True, they take risks and try new things. They continue to learn and refine their craft. However, these actions often stem from a sense of satisfaction rather than a desire to go out and do something innovative.

I used to think that contentment would make teachers complacent; that they would be taking bigger risks if they had nothing to lose. However, I've found the opposite to be true in my career. When I have felt the most content in what I'm doing I am more likely to take good risks. However, when I'm edgy and insecure, I actually grow risk averse.

Contentment can be difficult in teaching. Cafeteria duty can be loud and crazy and smelly. In some places, parents can be demanding. It can be hard to teach when kids interrupt you. All of these little things add up. However, a "dirty jobs" paradigm begins with the notion that all work is difficult, painful and boring at times, but that it's worth it if I get to do something that is challenging, meaningful, creative and autonomous.

One method that works for me is to reframe a difficult situation through a more grateful lens. For example, if I am stuck covering a class on my prep period, I can get really angry about losing the chance to plan for lessons. However, I can also see this as a chance to test out new ideas on a different class. It's a free pass to teach without the constraints of lesson plans or rigid curriculum guides. I can get upset about going to yet another assembly. However, I can also treat the situation as an opportunity to get to know students on a more personal level.

When faced with a stressful situation, I can recognize the reality that some things are outside of my control and therefore focus my attention on what I can change. It helps when I can consider the aspects of a crappy situation that also provide for autonomy, creativity, challenge or purpose.

## Realistically Optimistic

Expecting the job to be difficult doesn't mean we have to be pessimistic. Pessimism is often the result of unrealistic expectations involving the worst-case scenario. Case in point: I hate testing weeks. I get scared that my students will fail. I worry that our school will be shut down. I assume that students will be crazy when the test is over.

However, if I can think realistically about the test and recognize that, as evil as it might be, it will not destroy my school, my career or my students' lives, I can calm down and handle the situation with a greater sense of calm and even a touch of humor. By examining the facts (kids are scared, administrators are stressed, teachers are confused), I can create a more realistic plan of handling the situation. I can help my students remain calm. I can help them find a quality activity later in the day.

One strategy that has worked well for me during my most difficult seasons as a teacher was to create a journal of things that I am thankful for in teaching. I tried this for an entire year and began with the basics: a chance to change lives, a profession that lets me use my skills, a sense of meaning. Over time, I found myself being thankful for small things: the conversations with students in passing periods, the meaningful discussions we have regarding the nature of technology, little victorious moments inside of projects. In the midst of a hard time, this recognition of the good side helped me to remember that I'm lucky to have this job as a teacher.

I used to think that gratitude was something schmaltzy. I tossed it into the category of those motivational posters you get at the kiosk in the mall. However, I have learned that gratitude is gritty. It's realistic. It begins with the expectation that teaching will be hard. However, gratitude is part of what fuels my passion as a teacher. I remain here because, on a very deep level, I know I am doing something meaningful – and for that, I am one of the luckiest men in the world.

## Laugh a Little

This optimism and gratitude have ultimately led me to embrace humor as a teacher. Do I have a Darth Vader To Do List on my board right now? Why yes, I do. I believe there is power in humor. It was honestly a part of what kept me from burning out last year. It was a part of what kept the job fun. When you have a realistic, "dirty jobs" view of teaching, you can laugh a little. You are often surprised by the humor you see in your world.

I don't use sarcasm and I don't resort to ad hominem attacks in the name of "humor." However, I joke around often in class. It might be a wisecrack about pop culture, a musing on something ironic or the fun of wordplay. We have an area of the white board where students can create visual puns. Examples include "Everyone loves me. I'm the most poplar tree in the forest" or a picture of "Reese's Peanut Butter Cop," a candy dressed like a police officer. These visual cues help create a climate of humor. This wall is the first thing they see when they walk in the door. We laugh often in our class and the end result is a climate of joy. This sense of joy is a part of what fuels my fire as a teacher.

This, in turn, leads to higher student engagement. I have never seen a student doze off while laughing. It just doesn't happen. Well-timed humor can do to a lesson what it does to a book, movie or conversation - break things up. I would love to claim that all of my lessons are amazingly engaging. However, the truth is that there are lulls. Humor spices things up. This, in turn, allows me to enjoy my job. It's hard to burn out when you're having a blast.

I admit that it can be challenging to have a sense of humor in the midst of a really hard year. A teacher who is burning out is going to have a tough time stepping back and laughing. However, I had a rough year last year because of some issues with our school culture. I had one of the hardest years of my life.

However, I reached a point in the school year where I said, "I'm not going to stop laughing. I'm not going to let someone steal my sense of humor." I honestly feel like the ability to laugh was a part of what allowed me to go through a tough year and survive. I came to the realization that humor is deeply human. It's a necessity. I used to think it was just the icing on the cake. But then I thought about cakes and icing. Without icing, a cake isn't cake. It's sweet bread. It's a muffin. But add icing and it's one of the most beautiful things humanity has ever created.

Humor is a part of who we are. Ultimately, in the midst of a challenging situation, it is often what brings us back to hope.

## Fires Aren't Perfect

I love campfires. I love the warmth that they provide. I love the way they draw people closer together. However, if I'm going to be honest about it, campfires aren't perfect. I swear that wherever I choose to sit, the smoke tends to follow me. I can move around the fire but it's like it becomes possessed. The smoke billows toward me every time. Then there's the warmth factor. Sometimes I'm too warm in front of me and my back gets cold. Other times, I get bored in the moment and I yearn for a warm bed and a heated room.

And yet, I have never regretted a moment spent around a campfire. Between making s'mores and telling stories, I am struck by the fact that campfires are location of so many powerful, positive memories. When I walk away from a campfire, I am almost always reminded of what really matters – the people around me.

I could say the same thing about teaching. It's sometimes messy. It's often uncomfortable. Sometimes I'd just like a restroom break every once in awhile. And there are days when I swear the smoke is following me around. However, I have not regretted a day I spent in the classroom. What fuels me is the sense of purpose I get in what I am doing. As teachers, we are doing something that matters. We are doing amazing work.

## Reflection Questions

1. What is the relationship between realistic expectations and optimism?
2. Why are gratitude and contentment necessary for avoiding burnout?
3. Do you think contentment leads to complacency? Why or why not?
4. Do you agree that all systems are fundamentally imperfect?
5. What are you most grateful for as a teacher?

## Action Ideas

- Make a list of fifty things you are grateful for as a teacher.

- Keep a gratitude journal listing at least one aspect of teaching that you are thankful for each day.
- Write out your core beliefs about the world and humanity. Is it good? Bad? Both? From there, make a bulleted list of what the implications are for teaching, learning, discipline, classroom interactions, etc.

# Keep the
# Blaze Going

* * *

## Strategy #6:
## Embrace a community of trusted friends, where you can be open and vulnerable.

I'm an introvert. I prefer processing things alone first before I ever talk to a person. I tend to live in my mind. I push people away without realizing it because I thrive on space.

However, I need people. That might just be the most obvious statement in the book, but it's one that I forget. There are times when my fire was almost gone. I had a project that tanked. I shamed a student.

I had a hard time with an administrator. Those were the moments when I wanted to quit.

In those moments, I wanted to hide. I wanted to withdraw within and avoid people. It can feel embarrassing for me to admit that I need people. I can't survive as a teacher working as a lone ranger.

I think in the back of my mind I viewed burnout as a sort of contagious disease. I didn't want to bother people with the fact that I was struggling. What I now realize is that passion doesn't work that way. It's actually more like a wildfire. When I feel my fire dying and I go to another teacher who is thriving, I can lean on that friend and their passion spreads. In helping me, their fire actually grows. That's the power of community. When we have nothing left to give it is often the community that keeps the fire alive.

## Seven Reasons You Need to Reach Out

When I think about teachers I've known who burned out, I am struck by the fact that they toiled for so long in isolation. They didn't reach out for help. In many cases, they kept up the façade that everything was going just fine. That's why so often we are surprised by teachers who burn out. But the truth is that these burned out teachers needed community. In fact, we all need community. Here's why:

1. Challenge Your Thinking: Part of why we burn out is that we never make necessary paradigm shifts that will allow us to thrive. Reaching out to other people allows us to experience necessary conflict that can lead to those necessary paradigm shifts.

2. Remind You of Who You Are: Sometimes you forget who you are. Sometimes you define yourself based upon your actions rather than your identity. Sometimes you allow others to define you. This is why trusted friends are so powerful in this profession. They restore you by reminding you who you are.

3. New Ideas: Even the most creative teachers have blind spots when it comes to ideas. By engaging with a community, we get the chance to have fresh ideas and new strategies that will change the way we teach. This, in turn, keeps the flames alive.

4. Remind You of What You Believe: Sometimes we lose sight on what we believe about education. A trusted friend can gently remind us what we believe and why we believe it.

5. Help You Remember What Matters: Maybe it's test scores. Maybe it's the fact that you were stuck with cafeteria duty. Or maybe it's a parent who is suddenly annoyed with you and there seems to be no solution. Whatever it is, we tend to forget what ultimately matters in education. When we reach out to others, we are able to see with fresh eyes what things actually matter.

6. Affirm You: Teaching can be a thankless job. Sometimes we just need some affirmation. A trusted friend can provide that kind of encouragement.

7. Collaborate: I am working on projects with AJ Juliani. I am developing a digital publishing platform with Brad Wilson. These are things that fuel my passion and keep the blaze alive. However, none of this would work if I were doing this on my own.

## When the Community Isn't There

Ideally teachers would reach out to their colleagues. However, sometimes it is not safe to be vulnerable. Sometimes the culture is toxic and people respond to vulnerability by insulting others and spreading rumors. When work is no longer a safe place, it can be helpful to reach out to an outside community. Some people find this with their family, neighbors, longtime friends or religious community. However, it can also be helpful to reach out to a community of fellow teachers who can empathize with your experience.

This is part of why I love the idea of developing a PLN. I know PLN sounds like a kind of drug (not unlike LSD or PCP) but it's actually short for Personal Learning Network. For me, this community exists in blogs, on Twitter, on Facebook and on Voxer. Ten years from now, the platforms will have changed. However, the community will remain the same.

In the darkest moments of teaching, these connected friends saved my career. I remember hitting a point of burnout one year when nothing I was doing seemed to work. I was lost, struggling with how to manage a difficult class (it had been years since I had struggled so much with classroom management) and a new school environment. I was hitting a point where I no longer enjoyed showing up to work. My fire was fading.

I reached out to Jeremy Macdonald, because I knew that he was a safe person to be vulnerable with. During that time, I also reached out to Philip Cummings, because I knew he would empathize, offer wisdom and listen. I knew, again, that he was a safe person. I contacted Michael Doyle because he had known me for so long and he knew so much of my story. These people might sound like strangers but they were all friends I knew online. They encouraged me, listened to me, and ultimately helped me find my passion again.

I first got into the idea of a personal learning network, because I thought it was a place to learn. I would ask for lesson ideas or resources and I got exactly that. However, over time, things changed. What I now experience is a community of people that I care about. I can be open and vulnerable in ways that I can't do in a staff lounge. We can geek out over teaching theory without being told I'm being too geeky. I can celebrate a student success without feeling like I'm being arrogant. I can share my frustration without worrying that they'll think I'm a failure. We can laugh together. In some cases, we have cried together.

People are quick to call Twitter an "echo chamber," but that hasn't been my experience (at least not entirely). What I see are shared experiences and shared values. I disagree sharply with some people. However, we have so many shared experiences in the daily practice of being teachers.

And the power of the PLN is that I can share these experiences openly with trusted friends.

## The Power of Vulnerability

Transparency has become a buzzword in education circles. It's used to justify sharing one's data, talking about insights or simply being open about who you are. I've used it myself to describe my approach to online honesty. I'm starting to wonder if maybe transparency is a little cheap; if maybe it's a counterfeit for vulnerability, used to keep people just close enough without truly getting to know me.

Vulnerability is different. When you are vulnerable, you are able to share what is going on and openly admit that things aren't perfect. What happens next is people move in and grow closer. You are able to trust one another more. It is in these moments that you can lean on a friend when you have been knocked down.

In some cases, it can be helpful to be vulnerable in the classroom. As a teacher, you can let your students know that they have hurt you. Not in a whining way. Not in an accusatory way. However, in a very real, personal, strong way, you say to a student, "I was hurt by those words and I'd appreciate if you didn't get that route again." Nearly every time, they respond with humility.

Vulnerability also means apologizing when you screw up. Transparency would say, "This is what happened and here's why it won't happened again." Vulnerability demands a certain level of humility that cannot occur unless a teacher is willing to own up to his or her own humanity.

Teachers who are able to find a place to be vulnerable end up finding a place to be trusted. Over time, they grow as teachers. They improve in their practice. They are restored when they screw up. Their fire doesn't burn out.

## Reflection Questions

1. Do you agree that reaching out to others is critical to avoid burning out? Why or why not?
2. What has happened to you in the past when you were vulnerable? Did people reach out to you or reject you?
3. Who are the types of people you trust enough to share who you truly are? Who are the people you talk to when you are burning out as a teacher?

4. Have you ever been in a school culture where it was not safe to be transparent? If so, how did you handle that kind of situation?

5. What can leaders do to model vulnerability in their schools?

## Action Ideas

- Schedule a time to meet with a small group of teachers. Give yourselves the permission to "talk shop" and share what's really going on. But also give yourselves the permission to just go and hang without having to wear the "teacher hat."

- Develop a Personal Learning Network. Here are a few ways:
    o Find a platform. It might be Facebook, Google Plus, Pinterest or Twitter.
    o Find a community within the platform. For example, check the education-related chats that exist on Twitter. Find the groups that exist on Facebook.
    o Read blogs and begin writing a blog. Share it on social media. The education blogging community is often where ideas are shared and relationships grow.

# Maintain a
# Roaring Campfire

* * *

**Strategy #7:**
**Understand the phases of your career and**
**the potential burnout in each phase.**

Sometime in my fourth year of teaching, I stopped by another teacher's classroom. She was a veteran social studies teacher who taught with an energy and a passion that was contagious.

"I'm afraid I'm going to burn out," I declared.

"Are you having a tough year?" she asked.

"No."

"Are you wanting to quit?"

I shook my head.

"Then what's the problem?" she asked.

"I used to daydream about teaching. I used to plan lessons in my head while I was driving home from work. I used to get so excited about the start of a project that I couldn't go to sleep the night before. I don't feel that anymore."

"And that's a problem because?"

I didn't have an answer for her.

## The Phases of a Fire

It has me thinking about the fire metaphor. Every time we have a fire pit in our backyard, we start with kindling. It burns fast. It looks impressive. On the night that we use our old Christmas tree, the flame flies up toward the sky in a brilliant display of light. The kindling matters. It plays a role. However, it doesn't last. Ultimately, what matters is whether or not the logs catch fire.

As a new teacher, I made the mistake of focusing on the kindling. That initial excitement was the spark that allowed the fire to burn. However, it wasn't meant to last. It was novelty. It was fun. It flamed up in a way that was impressive. Meanwhile, the logs were just barely beginning to catch fire.

My current challenge is different. The fire has been burning for a few years now. I'm not consumed by what I am doing. I have set up boundaries that allow me to thrive. However, I am more tempted to grow bored and stagnant. If I'm not careful, my flame dies out. Sometimes it's helpful to think about a teaching career as phases of a fire with each phase bringing about new challenges and new opportunities.

## Phase One: The Kindling

In this phase, you work crazy hours. You are often excited about the work you are doing only to be alternately crushed by failure. The fire seems to be growing and then the kindling burns down and you find yourself adding to it. The truth is you are still learning how to be a teacher and the learning curve can be exhausting. It doesn't mean you're not amazing. It doesn't mean you are clueless about what you are doing. It's just that teaching is a craft that takes years to develop.

Challenges of this Phase:
- You can easily lose sight of what you believe. This is especially true when you are trying to prove yourself as a teacher. However, it also

happens when you take other people's advice too often or when you try too hard to fit in to a school culture.

- You can get so frustrated by your slow growth as a teacher that you begin to wonder if you should stay in the profession. You will have days that are so hard that they make you cry. Or, at least I did. That's right. I said it. I cried a few times my first year (and by "a few times" I actually mean "a whole bunch").
- You can allow the job to consume you and fail to take care of your basic needs.

Opportunities of This Phase

- You get to be energetic. Embrace that. It's a good thing. It will allow you to keep going even when it gets hard.
- You get the chance to dream like crazy. You probably have a bizzilion different ideas that you want to try out. Go ahead and do that. This is your chance to figure out what works.
- You are learning a ton. You are growing like crazy. This learning curve is pretty amazing.

Ideas for Thriving in this Phase

- Give yourself the permission to daydream in this phase.
- Remember your core values, beliefs and ideas about education. Don't let anyone take those from you.
- Forgive often. Forgive the students. Forgive the fellow teachers when they are standoffish or offensive. Forgive yourself when you screw up.
- Realize that failure will happen. Reflect on it and grow from it. Understand that the school year has phases as well. The exhaustion you feel in November isn't burnout. It's exhaustion. You're tired. The light is dying. It's getting colder. But you're not alone. Everyone wants to sleep in, drink hot chocolate and watch *Elf*. That doesn't mean you're not fit to teach. It just means you like hot chocolate and Will Ferrell movies.
- Find a mentor who can help remind you to build a steady fire.
- Remember that you need community and develop a PLN.

## Phase Two: The Flames Grow

You have started to settle down. Your energy isn't quite what it was before. The novelty has started to fade. The ups and downs are replaced with something a little more normal. The lack of novelty is replaced by a newfound expertise and confidence. You might be new but you know your stuff.

Challenges
- You are often tempted to try and keep up the pace you had in the Kindling Phase. You've made crazy work hours a habit and you may experience a level of guilt when you try setting up more boundaries.
- Boredom can creep in during the phase. You might find yourself getting restless.
- Although you are gaining expertise, some of your colleagues might still view you as a newbie and ignore your insights. This can be frustrating. Take it in stride and try your best not to tell them to "shove it."
- You will still screw up. This might make you angry, sad or even ashamed. You might feel like you should be over that by now. Just remember that you will never reach perfection.

Opportunities of This Phase

- You are far more knowledgeable now than before. No, it's more than that. You have grown in wisdom. You have a better understanding of what works in a classroom. Be confident in this wisdom.
- The ups and downs aren't as intense. From a purely personal standpoint, it's pretty cool to feel a greater sense of normalcy. I remember looking around and thinking, "Holy crap, I can breathe."
- If you are setting boundaries, you now have time to pursue things outside of school like knitting sweaters or training passenger pigeons.
- In many cases, you have earned more respect from the veteran teachers. In a healthy school, they are seeking out your ideas more often.

Ideas for Thriving in this Phase
- Give yourself the permission to work less even when others scoff at it. You don't get a sticker for working late.
- Go back to your core values, beliefs and ideas about education and make sure you are able to teach according to those.

- Sometimes teachers in this phase get complacent with what works. Remember to continue trying new things.

## Phase Three: The Flames Are Fading

In this phase, the coals remain alive even when the flames seem to be fading. The passion might not look as wild and energetic (though sometimes it does) as the Kindling Phase. However, there is a danger of complacency. There's a danger in a slow, quiet burnout.

Challenges

- Boredom tends to creep in. You've seen it all. If you're teaching middle school, I guarantee you that you've seen it all. At times, the job can feel repetitive.
- If you're not careful it can go from a career to "just a job."
- It is easier to get impatient with change; especially when it feels like there are ridiculous new initiatives. You have lived through every single fad. First, it was student notebooks, then writing across the curriculum, then Cornell Notes, then Word Walls, then Kagan Activities, then Marzano

Vocabulary, then Close Reading, then Text-Dependent Reading. You've seen whole reading, back to basics phonics and now blended reading. It's easy to get jaded and resist change.

Opportunities of This Phase
- You have gained a ton of wisdom. You have the chance to share that with new teachers. It might be the prime time to mentor someone.
- Your skill level is high enough that you can try a really challenging project and probably pull it off really well.
- You are able to see the big picture in ways others can't.
- You have seen enough of your former students (who have come back to thank you) that you are confident in who you are as a teacher and the fact that you are making a difference even when it is not outwardly obvious.

Ideas for Thriving in this Phase
- There are times in this phase that a teacher needs to change roles. It might be moving to administration or changing to a coaching

role. Sometimes teachers assume that this is burning out. It's not. There is nothing wrong with wanting to improve a school from a larger level. Similarly, there is nothing wrong with wanting to mentor new teachers and guide them along in their journey. That's not burnout because your passion is still there.

- Continue to challenge yourself in what you are doing. When things get boring, try something that will allow you to fail a little.

- Consider mentoring new teachers. If you have made it this far, you have probably had to reach out to other teachers during difficult moments.

- Take on a new project. Go do something bold and crazy and wild – just as long as it's not the kind that will get you fired.

## Keeping the Campfire Roaring

Each of the phases comes with a different set of challenges. These challenges can often feel like burnout in the moment. During the Kindling Phase, a teacher might feel burned out when it is simply exhaustion. During the Growing Flames Phase, a teacher might wonder if maybe he or she has lost the fire as teaching grows into a slower, steadier flame.

In the third phase, it can seem like you've lost your passion when the reality is that your passion simply looks different. In each phase, those challenges can eventually lead to burnout. However, when teachers are proactive, they can thrive in those phases.

One of the best ways to keep the fire roaring over the years is to keep things fresh. Try new ideas. Take on new projects that you hadn't considered before. I realized this as I was shifting from the second to the third phase. I knew that the student blogging and video projects were going well. However, I needed to teach something more challenging.

I started with the Geek Out Projects. Here students found topics that they were passionate about and developed their own multimedia packages on those topics. They engaged in research, chose their media and published their work for the world. I also had students try the Social Solutions project, which involved global collaboration on solving a context-specific social issue. Finally, I had students do a Shark Tank style project where they created a product, developed the marketing and pitched it to their classmates.

Ultimately, trying something new was a huge factor in avoiding burnout. It kept things fresh. It allowed me to continue to learn new things as a teacher. While this wasn't the single greatest factor in avoiding burnout, meaningful student projects were a major component of why I have continued to love teaching.

## Reflection Questions

1. Which phase would you say you are currently in?

2. What are your current challenges? How are you handling those challenges?

3. What are some of the opportunities you have right now? How are you managing those opportunities?

4. What are some ways that you are keeping your teaching fresh? What are some new ideas that you are trying?

## Action Ideas

Try something new. Create a project that you know will be challenging for you and force you to learn something new.

If you are new as a teacher, find a mentor who you can trust. The following are some characteristics that make a difference:

- Trustworthy: Is this someone who will keep secrets? Is this someone who will avoid talking crap behind your back?
- Compassionate: Does this teacher still care about kids?
- Available: Sometimes a great veteran teacher isn't available. It isn't personal if this person can't meet with you on a regular basis.

If you are a veteran teacher, consider mentoring a new teacher. Don't call it mentoring. Just offer resources, guidance and an open mind. The following are some ideas of what works in mentoring:

- Ask questions rather than giving advice.
- Find any expertise that a new teacher has (new theories, new ideas, etc.) and try one of those things out. New teachers often need to feel affirmed as much as challenged.
- Be open about areas where you are still failing. New teachers need to see the power of vulnerability.
- Offer to observe a new teacher's class and offer to let that teacher observe your classroom.

# Conclusion
## Reignite the Flame

I used to think that burnout was permanent. I thought that it was impossible for a teacher to go from feeling totally done with the profession to feeling passionate about teaching again.

I'm not so sure anymore.

See, I burned out last year. I never called it that. I think I used the term "hard year," but the truth is I burned out. The whole thing began when I was pulled into a meeting to talk about technology. Despite having a solid track record, we had experienced horrible wear and tear on a particular model of laptops. I felt entirely alone as I sat in an empty classroom for an hour and a half trying to explain why cheap technology fell apart.

I'm not going to go into the details but it was awful. I left the meeting in tears. I had never experienced that kind of professional shame in my entire career. I replayed every sarcastic comment in that meeting and wondered if maybe it really was my fault. Then I got angry at myself for letting it get to me.

I remember stopping my car in the parking lot the next day and having a panic attack. I was terrified and crushed and shamed to the core. I had to tell myself that I still liked teaching and I wasn't going to let fear define me. Still, things got worse for the next two weeks. I had never, in a decade of teaching, been the "bad teacher."

I was ready to quit. I simply didn't want to show up to work anymore. If someone had said, "John, I'll offer you twenty thousand dollars to quit teaching and go find something new" I would have taken it.

But I didn't quit. The situation improved slightly, but it was still difficult. However, slowly, my mindset shifted. I went from dreading going to work to tolerating going to work to falling in love with teaching again. Right now, I get up on just about every morning and look forward to being in the classroom. I went from burned out to thriving again in less than year.

## Surviving a Hard Year

The following is a list of ideas for surviving a hard year. If they seem similar to the ideas in the previous chapters, it's not an accident. The strategies that prevent burnout are also the ones that help a teacher pull out of it.

1.  Don't Let Shame Define You: Hard years have a way of humbling good teachers. In a hard year, a teacher will probably snap at someone or use sarcasm or yell at a class. Add to this a lack of outward results and it can feel humiliating. These horrible periods aren't horrible simply because they are uncomfortable. Rather, they are shameful and the only way to heal from shame is standing up and being unashamed. Sometimes that requires a trusted friend to remind you of who you are.

2.  Focus on Identity: During my hardest year, I hit a point in this process where I began to question who I was as a teacher. I knew better. I watched the work that my students were doing at the time and could point to it as

something observable. However, for all of my introversion, I found myself reaching out to two former principals who affirmed my identity as a competent teacher. I needed someone to say to me, "John, you don't suck at teaching."

3. Gritty Gratitude: One thing I missed in the midst of this period was that there were people on campus who had my back. Our assistant principal was amazing. I had a few co-workers on my team who were really there for me in the midst of it. However, I also had great classes with great students. All year, I kept a private thankful journal describing why I still loved teaching.

4. Try Something New: I know this sounds strange, but I have found that adding a new challenge can actually help in the midst of a hard year. When I had a difficult class, I found that focusing on developing a challenging project actually helped me refine my craft. This is how we ended up doing our videogame project on Scratch.

5. Redefine Success: In hard years, it's important to remember that you can control your actions, but not the results of the actions. It

helps to define success as faithfulness rather than results.

6. Find a Place to Be Vulnerable: Find someone who will listen to you talk about what's really going on and how you feel about it. This isn't venting. Venting is about bombastic blaming. Vulnerability is admitting that there is pain and anger as a result of circumstances. Vulnerability is saying, "It's actually really, really hard right now."

7. Blame the Circumstance and Not the People: It helps to remember that you work with broken people in a broken world. The fact that we manage to do as well as we do is actually pretty amazing. When I can focus on the circumstances and realize that the people are just as broken as me, I am more likely to find some real solutions that might work.

8. Set Boundaries and Then Find an Autonomous Space: Go paint a picture or write a novel or crochet a blanket. Go garden. Go glue macaroni onto something and spray paint it gold. Go find a space away from school, where you have total autonomy to excel in some creative act.

9. Humor: I laughed during that year. I didn't quit joking around with colleagues. I didn't quit drawing silly doodles on our whiteboard.

10. Focus on the Finish: It may be the end of the school year and it may be in a few weeks. However, this doesn't go on indefinitely. Simply knowing that it gets better allows me to plough through the hard days.

## Remembering What Matters

I mention all ten of those points above but to be honest there was a single moment that pulled me out of burnout in a profound way. It was a week after the horrible meeting with the principal. That night I opened up Facebook and streamed through a feed of teachers talking about how great things were going. I couldn't help but wonder if maybe I was delusional. Maybe I wasn't such a great teacher.

I thought about the global collaborative projects we did and how I presented the façade that they were awesome when in fact there were huge glitches along the way. I thought about the way I feigned expertise when there were so many things I was still learning.

That's when a name popped up in my friend request folder. I recognized the name and all I could remember was the time I had embarrassed him in front of the class and how I had met with him afterward to apologize. I accepted the friend request and a moment later, the chat button popped up.

"Mr. Spencer, it's me," he said. "You said you would accept our friend requests once we are out of high school. Well, I'm out of high school."

"How are you?" I asked.

"I'm in college now," he answered.

"Are you the first in your family?"

He answered with a grinning emoji. I knew his story. He wasn't just the first in his family to go to college. He was the first in his family to graduate high school.

"You still teaching?" he asked.

"Yeah."

"You still love it?"

"It's been a hard year," I answered. I didn't want to get into the "you can't handle technology" story.

"But you still love teaching, right?"

I sat there staring at my screen. I didn't know how to answer.

"Right?" he typed again.

I still couldn't answer him.

"Hey, I was wondering if I could be your student teacher. It's not for another year, you know. But I remember the way you taught. You made us think. I mean, you made us think hard. You remember making us do all that research?"

"I do," I answered.

"Well, I was wondering if you could show me how you teach that – you know the deep thinking stuff."

"Wow, thanks," I answered.

"You'll still be teaching in a few years, right? I mean you're not *that* old."

I stared at the screen again and found myself typing, "Yeah, I'll still be teaching." I was right. He was right. Even in the midst of a painfully hard year, I knew I wouldn't walk away. True, my fire was fading. It might have looked as though there is nothing left but ash. However, there was still a spark. Even on my hardest day in my hardest year, this moment was a reminder of everything that matters in teaching.

So I stayed.

# ABOUT THE AUTHOR

John Spencer is a middle school photojournalism and computer teacher in urban Phoenix, Arizona. Over the last eleven years, he has taught social studies, language arts, language acquisition and technology, along with his experience in professional development and teacher coaching. He is a frequent keynote and conference speaker who recently delivered an address at the White House Future Ready Summit.

His research experience includes writing a chapter in *The Nature of Technology* textbook and winning the NAU Education Technology Graduate Award for his work around transforming professional development.

Spencer is an avid writer whose work has been featured in *Kappan Magazine, The Answer Sheet,* and *Edutopia.* He is the author of *Wendell the World's Worst Wizard* and co-founder of Write About.

Blog: spencerideas.org
Twitter: @spencerideas
E-mail: john@educationrethink.com